Badinfinity.

poems

Brian
Townsley

---

guerillalit
los angeles : new york : san francisco

www.guerillalit.com
fight for it!

guerillalit would like to thank
the litmags, sites, walls, and
message boards in which some of
these poems and stories
originally appeared.

Cover art & icon by Tim
Townsley.
(www.timtownsley.com)
Book design by guerillalit.
© 2007, Brian Townsley
ISBN: 978-0-6151-6530-1

Contents.

Bad
        in
    fi
              ni
    ty.

The dreams are real.
A bygone necessity
dictates their arrival, the song
you cannot rid yourself of.
None of the time I sit
drinking coffee
in the café breathing
the dawn forward
changes the facts,
however I rearrange them.

So I make the ink blood
& paint the walls with it,
slung about like Pollock
on ecstasy, like heartbreak
without recovery. It's
the best thing going, dancing
the 26 to their death,
night and night again,
like dreams unwanted,
catharsis,
retelling the truth
with lies.

There is no past, there is only
story. And though I have
kissed the immortal lips
of Aphrodite, the fates
would have it otherwise.
The same bygone necessity

grown rhythmic & tired, this
memory, this atlas
of bones.

I await the night.

The river awash in offsuite
odds & elementary subtraction,
the result of which leaves
the under of nothing. There would be
no forgiveness this time,
she will shake her head & hips
like a dashboard ornament
(of course, she is) given awful
consciousness, god was in his cups
the day he
granted that. I ran my hand over
the table as I left, the last time
I'd feel shaved felt,
the pleasure there. The dogs of
lament followed me home, past
junkyards & accordion shops &
love songs for diamonds that
crooned of old glory & the madness
of the turn. My pockets were
empty outside
car keys & a dried sunflower
I'd fondled for luck. The jazz of
chance skittered across the pavement
& I thought of my doll at home
in the car, how she sleeps
with the owner because she's stuck
to the dash with tape,
doublesided & though she leans
left and does not play her ukulele
loud enough to hear, her
fate is undeserved like the last

hand on the last day. The car is up
ahead, parked at a meter where she's waiting
for my newest failure, the cards that
wouldn't turn. I will blame the
Chinese government for the cards
they make in tiny shops there, how
they are biased against
genius, this fire in my hands. I stole her
from the dollar store, she's never let me
forget it.

One.

the dead ache for
the time
you waste.

The Painter

Hung on the walls
with synonyms like bent nails
hammered into studs
the gaze of Beckett, Joyce,
Yeats, O'Neill, charcoal
on paper, oil on canvas.
I grew up here, amid
the open eyes of art and
the adaptability of plastic,
how so like skin
we show off our work
these plastic tits & jawlines
plastic tans & beneath
deeply injected like
Waiting For Godot
                the plastic soul.
But the paradox is expected.
The sun sets here.

Thank God for Jameson &
Bushmill in the trunk
the respite there.
              Here in the gallery
my father the artist
stands about his work and
comes to realize
that the new movement
the next generation
in art
is plastic. Him, surrounded
by four Irish writers, so many

sets of eyes, the only creature
savagely natural
like a stud farm for
the talented & unlucky.

They lay strewn about the floor
like so much spilled birth
all stained placenta and
smeared fluid like ink
on folded paper
these tiny abortions are meat
from the fruit of loathing &
perceived pain & whiskey
& the wailing sparrow of blue ruin.
I pick from among the quartered bodies
those things left behind. The hymn
of water long forgotten,
the hairline of my father,
choices exacted from the
bloody remains
some of which resemble
the buds of flowers
others not so much. They are dead
hours and always the bruising.
Some misshapen in exquisite
human loneliness, some in need
of stitches and a smoothing out
they will never receive
for the swagger home. There are nights
I am awash in them
their inadequate organs & incomplete
perfection having loved too deeply
the bad angels within.
But the dead still hope.

It is this to be a man. Insufficient

for these failures, unequipped for
the powerless wail
the depth of pain nature afforded women.
I howl at my failed creations
they do not answer back.
I buckle inside at such things. Enough
to impress the fragility of those birds
in hand, the son a sanctuary of
second life, that bottled rhythm of
bound speech that finds a canvas
upon which all hope hinges.

Away from college for
the summer job
arranged by a booster, the wonder
of connections the miracle
rubbed raw. It was
a paint company in Downtown
Los Angeles & the city
held her head in her
hands that July. I drove the 10 down
inching my way with the rest
of them, & would get
the daily duty from
the owner.

First I went to hardware stores
& superstores
Home Depot & the like
setting up displays, moving
signage & pallets & paint cans
in Gardena, Monrovia, West Covina,
fingers of LA & her trains.
They said I did well, that
I could display the product
like a man with talent.
It went on like that, me choosing
to play the game, the chip
on my shoulder evident to
the blind. Not that I was proud of
my performance or
the job, rather
I was destined for greatness

&
that shameful knowledge
brought no enlightenment.

After work I would park
at Union Station
and watch the trains come & go,
the stutter & hard rhythm
of somewhere else.

One day I arrived and there were no more
displays to put up. Southern California
was colonized & I had run
the fucker. It was the factory
for me, the summer's remainder
like an ink stain on the new shirt.
I began that day, filled pallets with
paint cans, switched to the conveyer
the labels there. I placed the labels on the cans
& snapped the handles into place. The old
Mexican next to me was much quicker
he had a system.
At the cart at lunch
he explained that he had
been putting handles onto cans for
25 years
& was looking forward to his retirement. Manuel
showed me pictures of his kids &
wanted to hear about the football. After lunch,
my performance got worse
rather
than competent.

I struggled through the week &
then another
ended & the boss called me into the office.

He fired me
for being too slow on the assembly line
claimed I lacked passion
that there were no hard feelings
but he had to let me go.

I had never been fired before
& found it shameful &
liberating. I drove to the tracks to
watch the trains. I didn't
want to go
home, didn't know what to say.
So I watched the trains.

Later my mother told my grandfather
that I had been fired
that factory work had proved
my undoing. The next time
he saw me, he took me aside, said
thank god they tanked you. I wouldn't stand
for my grandson working
in a factory. Don't worry,
it just means that you won't stand
for that bullshit. You've got
bigger things planned. I'da been
disappointed if you hadn't a been
fired. He smiled and slipped me a twenty
and that was that.

My grandfather wore suits on off days &
lived a life of chance &
bet the house on poker nights
to bend the branches so the gods
could watch. I took the twenty &
set fire to the night.

The map on his hand will
decide the path, the angles
and necessary negotiations
measuring the humanity, its
given length.

The man is hung like
a ballad, like loss sweetened
to charity, like the last stagger
of the boar mined
in buckshot and roar.
But he will make the trip
below
the moon's sailing
grace like an exercise
in farewell, the remembered routes
like lovemaking all
similar and never the same
days bleeding to years
yet every morning
the stunned dawn
the pockets of meaning
sadly raided.

Never mind the death that awaits.
Take vitamins
& supplements jeweled
in the darkness &
master rhetoric
the only friend you will have,
the Taoist/agnostic/philosopher

advises
but he is baby's breath &
does not recognize sarcasm.

Beware those who read
the fine print.
Take comfort in the inevitability
of it all, the alchemy
of marrow & faith &
the soil weak with roses.

Upon autumn's back the leaves
stack the gutters and
the angels condemn
the holy.

Love Song

So many things pass
inescapably
away.

I think of those years
in Berkeley
and they are distilled
to a point so fine
there is no resemblance
to history but rather
remembrance
of acute detail without
accuracy, the only truth
in a house
of lies. It is always raining
I am living on $2 a day
walking to school
because
parking is impossible and
gas too expensive. A bagel
at Andronico's
sets be back .65
but will last me through noon.
Classes and notes and rain
and white rice with teriyaki sauce
at Yokahama Station, another
dollar down, to practice
then home and dinner
beans and tortillas
and homework
calling the girlfriend

and then writing the book
the worst book
ever put before the gods.
But there were moments.

Chuck Bailey calls them
comebackers on the golf course, and
while I have few of them there
I wouldn't be here
if not for that novel.
The place on Alcatraz,
the place in Albany, the nights
in bookstores—
Cody's, Moe's, Serendipity, Shakespeare
& Co., Pegasus, Black Oak, Cartesian,
University Press. And still, the rain.
Come to think of it
it didn't always rain
but in this poem
it did.

The collected Joyce for $2 was a
particular find and then
the obligatory trip to
the café,
the Mediterranean,
La Scala. Coffee Au Lait
and the opening of covers
spanning
netherworlds unimagined
like Clifford Brown on
Blue Note
like *The Bear*
something tiny but crucial
and in it
the raging power of

my beloved city
itself.

Upon Returning
for RKJ

You were bleeding inside
upon landing at LAX, back
from China, unable to leave
the sacred red in
your formidable history. I recall
the heart trouble as you lay
across the red Czech crest
in Prague, some years ago.
That red you tried to leave behind.
The voices you hear trumpeting
your years here, echoes
of the young Chet you played with.
They are memories, not
madness. Now redfaced and
bleeding from the mouth
that scar unclosed, fated
like Lancelot the spilling of
youth recalled from discord,
stitched and unstitched so many times
and beyond repair.

Go to the country
to get healthy.
I wish you luck. The China
that has stayed with you
and tipped your shoes red,
the Czech that is always there.
Red flames burn the valleys
on this red red morning,
there is water for that.

The blood on your handkerchief
will not wash off.

the banners of the dead

we do not stop
for the fallen
nor speak of them
it is not us
not ours
not anything of worth
nothing
but a moment of silence
while we sip our $5 coffee
and think of our next fuck
under the draped flag
in the dead wind
hung for ideals as foreign
as oil
as war
as death.

My son sits in the basket &
eats grapes while I push
the cart about the supermarket.
Eggs, beer, cheese, broccoli,
some yogurt for the little
one. A bag of chips. They all
collect about him like
days of chance. He
does not waste a thought
on the allover
hopelessness, the weeping
then & now
of the planet. He picks up
the green beer bottle
and looks through it
at me. The lady fondling onions
like balls glances at me
& back at his 4 years & the beer.
She shakes her head. So
much easier to cast
the sentence to the next man. I say nothing
to her about the face
she was born with,
the potato sack
she presents herself in. How she
handles onions. The terror
the men in her life
have put up with. But my son
has touched a beer
and thus
I reek of the darkest

laughter.

The ordered madness of row
upon row of plastic
encased preservatives &
cardboard boxes is itself
a preliminary exercise on
the bureaucracy of hell.
I push the cart through
the aisles
for the coming meals. I think
of poetry, the next book, the
novel I need to get back into. I have my doubts
The Pushcart Prize will be won
by the elements
of this errand, but I've got
the real thing here,
buddy. Top that.
Spam & Cheez Whiz for
everybody.

Dostoevsky in a '53 Pickup

The rain tonight is tying down the heavens
with vertical lines like puppet strings
like a bar code
the tattoo I saw on the neck of a young man
today running through the cloudburst
as if the drops themselves were cancer
causing scanners and he the purchase.
It is rumored that Dostoevsky's brother,
Mikhail, was drowned
in vodka
by his own serfs. And here,
only rain.
The palm trees in Southern California
have always looked like the world's largest
flowers and their sway
belongs underwater thus
their comfort this evening.
I am at home in the mystery
of things, their singular mythology
the unknowing there.
In *House of the Dead* Dos
rails against rational egoism with the widow
near the prison camp, her
very existence a poke in the eye
to those pesky rational egoists but
despite this critical analysis
I cannot keep from staring at the poster
in my room
the portrait of W. there
the satanic pin on his collar
and the rivulet of blood from the corner

of his mouth settling
on his chin. It's quite becoming
along the lines of
soiled sheets & rancid pork.
I do not drink as much
as I claim in my writing and my writing
is not as good as I claim.
But there are maladies yet to be sung
and so much narrative still unread
in bathroom stalls—in Berkeley alone
you could waste a month. And Dos
would fit nicely in the cab
of a '53 Chevy Pickup, three on the column
and brakes that lock over twenty.
No matter,
it will get him to the tables.
Interesting to me
that the first existentialist
a compulsive gambler. But then
he had lost his mother, father, wife,
& brother by that time
so a '53 and a roundabout
at the casino we'll afford him.
We'd even spot him a few large
if we could afford it.

I've got a bag of angels
in my pocket
today,
a tangerine
of a woman downstairs
who wonders
why I am here
and not there.
No answer for that.
Life is a painful melody
worth singing
through—listen to nothing
different.

this is a poem about growing up

Autumn has sprung loosely
into winter like the five pounds
you will gain for padding. These are
the rules, you do not
have to like them.
Compass points
for the road home, as it were.

And it is. Thus the mapless twenties,
the panic that follows like so many
fruitless epiphanies, the spirit
under the staircase. You bury it there,
knotted, like a half Windsor, like
the practicality of coffee cans. So many
options and none of them involve
the coffee.
           This is the way we live,
the proof and prescriptions that
get us through the night.
The reasoned ability to
ignore. Go easy
through the winter, she was
made to be more than
simply frigid, the mathematics of
the brittle vineyards piercing
the skin &
soil, crunching with frost
in the early morning.
Each billow
of breath shaped
with last nights scotch &

that which will not be
forgotten.

Have faith that we have your best interests in mind.
Have faith that we are one of you.
Have faith that we only make laws to protect you
from you.
Have faith that your son is now with God.
Have faith that The Rapture will arrive before the
polar ice caps melt.
Have faith that we won the election.
And the second one.
Have faith that we are the beacon of democracy
throughout the world.
Have faith that we are safer with Saddam Hussein
headless.
Have faith that we are not at war for oil.
Have faith that your daughter is now with God.
Have faith that the Bill of Rights is being
downsized for your protection.
Have faith for fear of being unpatriotic.
Have faith that God is on our side.
Have faith that the Indians were savages.
Have faith that the insurgency is on its last legs.
Have faith that Kenneth Lay died of a heart attack
shortly before he was to go to prison.
Have faith that being sent back involuntarily to the
front line makes us safer in the war on
        terror, even as a National Guardsman.
Have faith in your president.
Have faith that your God is stronger than Allah,
Zeus, Buddha, the Tao,
        and L. Ron Hubbard.

Have faith that we never lie, and when we do, it is
for your protection.
Have faith that your husband is now with God.
Have faith that the needs in Iraq were more pressing
than those in Iran, North Korea, East
        St. Louis, and Washington, D.C.
Have faith that W. is a man of the people.
Have faith that you would feel comfortable talking
sports with him at a coffee shop.
Have faith that that is what you want in a president.
Have faith that Social Security will still be there for
you.
Have faith that your father did not die for oil.
Have faith that you don't need to read to learn.
Have faith that gas prices will level off.
Have faith that the middle class is not disappearing.
Have faith that home prices will level off.
Have faith that we believed in WMD's.
Have faith that we would not send you into harm's
way for our personal interests.
Have faith in the system.
Have faith in the pharmaceutical industry.
Have faith in what you are told.
Have faith in the American way.

Writing my cousin
in prison
serving a life sentence
is far more difficult
than
writing
poems.

There is nothing to say
about things that matter
I don't know
what they'll cross out
don't know
what they'll allow
don't know
what he wants to hear.
My job is fine;
wife, son, healthy.
The poems are what they are
and
the weather has cooled to
the low 30's in the morning.

There is a guilt
somewhere
for living the things
he is not able
while I
steal the language
and play the hand dealt
as he does.

I write of the gods
and fate
as if they are things
more than
pitiful error
and
the smashing of time.
The clock behind me ticks
and again
and I stretch
relaxed
think of what tomorrow promises
what injuries
what mystery
there.
And if none of this holds
this poem
this night
this thought
the consequences
thereof.
We're all beaten
whether by ourselves
or others
but
the bull in the ring
the aging whore
the hospital patient
the man in a cage
have something
unwanted
&
so primal—
they know the luck has passed them by;
the rest of us

haven't figured that out
yet.

My friend Tobias drove home
last night drunk and topping
the gauge at over 100mph.
He is trying to kill himself,
or actually live, it is
confusing. Beckett
would know the difference.
Immature
perhaps for a man of more
than 40 years, but think of
what you have done. Now
think of what you haven't.
No time yet for your
hundred indecisions. The day wasted
memorizing *Prufrock*
& staining the baseboards.

My mother is a cancer
survivor. The unwanted
inheritance.   My grandfather
thought that Mexicans smelled funny and
that blacks lacked intelligence
but
managed a successful business
throughout his lifetime, lucky
enough to win & then
lose 50 grand in a poker game
in Vegas
in 1965. Of course, the country
was going to shit about then
so he figured why not

expedite the process
for the family. My grandmother
didn't speak to him for days.
He returned the gesture
after she voted in
Tom Bradley for mayor
of Los Angeles, he being a black man
and my grandfather figuring
her ballot canceled his.
We'll assume Herbert didn't vote
for Bradley. 40% of those who fall
off a horse are drunk while falling.
I expect I would fall off a horse
stone sober. I own a pair of cowboy
boots though.

Bob Hope fought under the name of
Packey East, Dino under
Kid Crocett. I'd have loved to see that bout
circa 1970. My father sparred for beer money
and was knocked black by Jerry Quarry, who
went on to lose to Frazier and Ali
and was unable to dress or
feed himself at the end. I have received
my mother's innate cooking ability with eggs.
My son has been passed the gift of
mapreading. My family
is extraordinary. Like yours.

I went to the eye doctor for an exam
and he prodded and covered one eye
and asked what I saw. He showed me
pictures in various hues
and made me look through blurry
lenses. He was bent over and walked
like Renfield and blew air at my

45

retina for fear of glaucoma and
blindness. It was clear he was looking
for something. Then he sat in his chair,
hunched, and spoke: you have
perfect vision. It has deteriorated
from 20/16 to its current 20/20, come back
in ten years when you need reading
lenses. He knew it was a matter of time
so I asked:
why not just give me
glasses now, since they have already
begun their rot? I smiled. He
smiled. It is all a waiting, the world
a graveyard of those things
unsaid
&
undone.

My German grandfather lost the eldest son
in Vietnam, and his death spread itself across
two decades. He died speaking of memories
none of us knew existed
in an old folks home tended
by blacks and Mexicans. There is poetry
in that, though *the best of the best American poetry*
will never recognize it.
The stories worth hearing are a retelling of
the truth. One does not preclude
the other though it need not include it.
But you know that. You know well
that poems and yarns meant to confuse
are facsimiles of the writers failures, that
the truth is blunt and
quick. The dead ache for
the time you
waste.

In the room below the women come and go
and speak not of Michaelangelo
but instead the shadow on the mammogram
and the fake Chanel bag
from Venice beach. 10% of men are
left-handed, only 8% of women. There must
be something to that. No one in my family
is a lefty besides me. From whom did I
inherit that genius? Will they mount
my head upon the wall
in the game room and recall
the sea-girls wreathed in chemo
and couture to laugh amid the
snap-shut of the zippo?

Two.

it rained the sky loose
         like the analog
      static of a record
              player.

The snow is still falling outside
it is mid-April
and the sky is heavy & opaque when
there is sky at all. The rest of the time
the heavens lick the pavement
with fog so thick
travel is useless. It is easy
to think of vacation
at a time like this, Mexico
perhaps. But I was just there
and it is no better.
Rosarito. Many
of the things I dislike about America
were in Rosarito
and very few of the things
I like about Mexico.
We brought back the simple truth,
little sleep, and handmade bracelets
for my 3-year old's friends. The four hours
to cross the border
they don't give back.
No wonder they hop the fence and run.
No waiting there.
And the border agent grilled
my son in the back seat
to make sure he belonged
to us.
He had to answer questions
about who we were,
about preschool. We talk so much
and get it all wrong

and hear no evil
only to read the headstones
for those things unsaid.
We are graceless & tuneless
and deserve so much worse
than we get.
All of us.
I saw the whole of it in the eyes of the coyote
this morning
on the drive to work. We made
eyecontact as he waited for
for my car to pass, for the centuries
to pass. Johnny Cash
was singing
mama said the pistol was the Devil's right hand
and the snow was falling
and the coyote
waited in silence for winter to die.
I will never
understand
anything.

it has always seemed to me
boys playing with guns
plastic ones
or armed
with caps that smelled
of sulphur
in the unsolvable
argument,
the beast of nature
that sits upon
the soul of man
without rest.
It lays in wait
for
old men seeking
profit from the spirit of
the young, the seam
that ties each of us
one to another.
Each XY
waiting for the justification
to kill.
It never tires, though
the flesh sags,
the music fades,
the astonishment
feasts upon itself
in rot.

Perhaps it is the true nature,
the gist is only

the darkened cycle
without resolve.
Men breathe in flowers
& female like laughter
without end
& exhale
to hack out the pestilence
inside each of us.
The old men
smile of Ares and dream
of dogs sharpening their teeth
on the bones
of the
fallen.

Spring has swallowed winter whole
and spit out the spine about these mountains
amid the heresy of rain and flooded
tributaries. As I stood on the deck
tonight blind as fortune
afraid my thoughts might shatter
the glass stars pendant
the first stars in some time
but I remembered them anyway
each fragment and collapse
a diamond
in my mind like fact
like 40,000 Americans were injured
last year by toilets
got me thinking
about the dangers of the necessary
but then
we keep death row inmates
                    on suicide watch
and only give patents to pharmaceutical
companies who create chemicals
in laboratories and ban natural products
that heal
they are trying to control
the way we die.

So use the toilet all you like. It's risky
but so is valium and vicodin and
that ache that won't go away
amid the impersonal riot
of night. The bent angle of light

on my deck from the open door
calls ecstatic
in its lamentation.
When I add it all up
like years
it begins to hurt.

on a photo of cadets at VMI reading Howl

Their hats lay crowndown
upon the desk
and in each hand a pocket poet
genius babble portable & still
inappropriate as an obscenity
trial. One future officer
cradles his forehead
in silent thunder like any student
in any classroom
he did not expect to have to conquer
the concept of irony
and discover
himself a sacrifice to
Moloch (from Leviticus, and
Sunday mornings, he
recalls the name but
little detail)
all before lunch.

like a python swallows a dog whole

I was 8, maybe 9, and
he was thicker by at least
5 years. He was walking with three girls
unimaginable then as now
one whom I thought of when
the thoughts had no handle to them
as I walked alone.

I said nothing to any of them. Did
nothing
to draw attention besides
being alone.
I was walking home from
elementary school and as
I turned the corner
he sprung at me.
I fell
on a front lawn and
he straddled me, punching
madness and childhood
alike
outweighed by 40 lbs
& fear. I had yet to catch
my breath
and behind him
the three girls
laughing & embarrassed. They
wore an expression like
they wanted to help
but didn't.

He finished & threw my backpack
across the street amid
the small inhumanities.
The punches didn't hurt, the backpack
was retrieved. But the shame
of having it done
in front of the girls
I feel now.

I think his name was Ricky. And
I still walk home
sometimes. He's welcome
to try again.

There is no opening line
worse than this. The curtain raised
to the ache and squeal of
arthritic pulleys, the stage
empty. The red night passing
for a spotlight reminds me of
London, though I've yet
to go. I spent a few hours
at Heathrow once, the exchange
rate exhausted me. Airports & hospitals
being facsimiles for existence
thus
the expressions *dead time, holdover,*
life support. It's like
confessing to a 12-stepper
dating the prom queen
fucking on the beach
all marvelous ideas until
the ride home. So anyway,
no London.
And the sparrows are silent
tonight, the red heavens, loosely
folded in maroon drapery amid
the balancing of luck & scar tissue
Above, the raised eyebrow
of the infinite. For there is
no punch line to the gods better
than a man's plans. Their laughter
breaks diamonds & smothers children.
The red sky
is having its way tonight

mainlining bad ideas,
playing the part of orator
at a funeral. I am in the front
pew, I cannot leave
cannot escape to Paris
or Prague or London.
It will last as it lasts.

party scene

Rarely do your movies contain
violence relying instead on
the cold snap of December
the death of the spirit long before
the failure of skin and tissue.
The last scene,
the cocktail party, and the room there
blackened down and backlit
in red and laughter. The portrait
of the father above the fireplace
speaks in obscene clichés to each
passerby, a man naked
from the waist up hatted with an
Aztec mask offers crab cakes
on a steel tray
held like a child. The stain
on the carpet has matted
the fiber in burnt crimson
and spreads with conversation.
You pan the walls and the
beautiful useless things there,
all bottled napalm and mink
underwear. I am in the corner
the bad idea given teeth
spilling my drink and insulting
the guests who wait in line
for their turn at originality.
I am the lion's roar
they hoped to hear the serenade
of acid & wit &
vacuity.

The elevated television
unleashes explosions of soil
soldiers in distress
compressing their helmets
and vomiting on themselves
in foxholes. You stay
behind the camera
as if
you are the only one
ever to be let down.

Outside the loft
the multitudinous rain
wild sermon of heresy
puppeteering the sane.
You knew
I was perfect for my role
& the critics
& timeclocks
& sparrows
concur.
The debutante's wailing
is ambiguous madness and
laughter while the camera zooms
on her teetering artifice of careful
humanity, the darkness
of her opened mouth.

This night is wrapped in fist &
conscience unheeded. They say that it may
snow tonight, but I believe
in their ability to be
wrong. No I do not steal
from Goodwill, no
I do not know how the stain
got there, yes my dog is buried
in the backyard, no I will not
dig him up
to show you.

Suppose our fear of the
dark is valid. What then? There
can be no success with
this, this dream
buried in the shoebox beneath
my dog. I walk to the window
and I still
don't believe them. No
snow tonight. No
the ink stains do not come off
they blur
but never leave. Like the
best of us.

The rest of us bury the minutes
like zoo animals bored
with being only
animals, so flick our feces
on the watchers for

amusement. Yes this crap
is for you, yes
I am staring at you, no
you are not forgiven, no
I will not
cooperate.

It takes the savage discipline
of a monk
to avoid a life in cliché,
the next line
the fashion in a casino
the statues of the corrupt
& deadly.

Our elected officials are the point
of the knife we sit&spin
upon, their ravages & excess
a perpetual astonishment to the
masses, the brainless repeated
while dogs sleep on sofas
made in China
or kiln dried in North Carolina.
They are not fooled.

The World Series is on
downstairs, eighteen men
in baseball hats & supplements.
My prediction is this:
one team will win, another
will lose.   One city will riot while
another will beat their wives.
Both cities will burn at the seams
because uneducated millionaires
have bested each other
on a baseball diamond
to laugh about it later
over an 18 year old

single malt.

This is what we care about.
It is our fault.

Thus the tailored suit today, if/when
things go awry.

The NSA is collecting phone records
to catch the terrorists among us.
Sniffing at the jungle's rim
for the spiked pheromone
the panicked animal
never mind the civil protections
the smoke prayers
the democratic process.
I don't call many people, they
should be concerned about the numbers
I don't call.
And my conversation last Thursday
with my father concerning
the Dodgers game.
Was that of particular import? The bomb
that did not detonate,
Nomar's liner surprisingly short
but
we are not trolling the lives
of innocent Americans
the operative word being
innocent. Before or
after the tap?
Because our topics may include
(but are not limited to)
Joyce, Beckett, Cheney's ballsack,
Iraq, Iran, the Gulf Coast,
the Dodgers, Cheney's hunting ability,
my mom's birthday, de Kooning,
bottled water.
Surely some treason

can be found there.
An old professor of mine
was quoted as saying that W.
is a man of humanity and compassion who
cares about human suffering.
He is clearly concerned
about his phone tap as well.
My professor never
mentioned his dementia in class
but there you have it. And while you're
taping and recording
take my trash out please
and I have a yard full of dogshit
real WMD's
compile those for your records
or
use them as chalk for
your new foreign policy.

I am the rabbit pinned in the jaws
of the tophatted wolf
but the hunted still hope.
I wish I was in the New Orleans
I knew
not the present day Atlantis
the administration
has allowed it to become.
Walk Perdido
through the quarter, take in
an au lait and plate of beignets
at Café Du Monde. If only
foreign oil meant less
than American lives, classic
American cities
undressed now like Dresden.
Our gas prices lengthen like

Pinocchio's nose pushing a dry drunk
to its limit and balancing his
dunce cap shaped like the arc
of an empire, the fated crescent
bent in arrogance
and ignorance soaked deeply
in the soil
and sewage still rising.

You, sir, have written your verse
in a child's scrawl
as a cheap hustler for God
and made me ashamed
of my country.
There can be no recompense
for that. The cold ground
awaits the masters of war
and cowboys alike,
and patriots count the
days.

lament

It is
innate
a virus
that reeks
of
humanity
rotted down
the centuries
our
allotted time
eaten
away by the
cancer
that sits
in our
bones
and
consumes
the athlete
the artist
the banker
the taxman
the student
the teacher
the priest
the believer
the atheist
the juggler
&
the dwarf:
the undefinable

want
of more
than we
are
capable.
And for that
the gods
swallow
us
whole
and shit
out
the mediocrity
of our
lives.

lullabye for the deaf

The typewriter clacks into form
another failed piece, another
attempt at something more than
poetry
while the song I am listening to
bleeds the night open
and endows the listener
more than words,
more
than rhyme scheme and alliteration.

What I want
is to learn a new language,
to hear more than
blown embers westward
or
collapse of red twilight,
more
than what I have to give.

I look down at my hands, unable
to pluck a string,
they cannot even
paint what does not translate.
They know the piano part
by heart but cannot play it.
They know only
the tired dance of the 26.

The song has left me on
the darkened streets of

The City, rain-slicked in skin
of wet pavement and the elegaic
spin of tire. You'll learn to flip your
collar at this point, near the bridge,
when the pace picks up. Hum
the chorus, this braille
for the night.

death in California

My aunt died when I was a teen
I am unsure now as to why
I am sure that I didn't ask then
but we collected in her room
and stood over her
around the bed
on which she had smashed
the anvil
and
the adults had things to talk about:
death, mortgage payments,
funeral expenses and the rest,
and they left me
in the room
with her.
Unattached.
I realized I was alone
and sat in a chair next
to the bed and looked upon her
for the first time.
She was waxy
but otherwise untouched
by the pale hand
and
damned if I didn't believe
that she would sit up
and talk to me
at any moment, hell
maybe tapdance
for a bit before making
the final edit in

the fine print of
the finite.
The entire family on that side
had moved from Boise
to Los Angeles pinning
their hopes on my aunt
being the next
Shirley Temple.
Clearly
that didn't work out
but she died just the same.
I didn't want to leave her
side then, afraid
that my absence
would somehow upset
some balance that had been
negotiated with the gods
in my head.
But the thought of her sitting up
was too much and I fled
the scene to eat the appetizers
on display in the living room
and watch the living humans
there.

I also threw lemons at my dad's dog
when I was 8
and he was recovering from
surgery after being hit by a car.
The kid across the street
influenced me
but I don't blame him
he was always an asshole
and I knew better. The dog
was a Newfoundland, a 150 lb.
beast with an upright carriage

who, when healthy,
could have
swallowed me whole
and shat me all over the yard.
He never did recover
and died shortly thereafter.
I don't think it was the lemons
but the moment has always
bothered me
a small cross for a small boy
cut of dogwood and lemon tree
and my own inadequacy.

The events share little but
me
and death in California
and those holes
never filled.

sometimes, courage
is the only swing left
in the darkness. Like a dram of
small poison the waters of life
are enough to push
back against
the dying, to hold off
the coming early darkness
of winter
& the long road home.

Let's hope that
it's interesting, that it's
not as we're told
that
the stories are more than
simply warm breath
on the cooling
corpse. Put your blind heart
to the earth
& how it pounds back,
matching
life for life.

There cannot be more than
wind & rain & art
& the majesty of
her smile
or else
the myths
have taught us

nothing. Repose.

It is me humming in
the dark night, me
washing out to sea
me
saving a haymaker
&
a kiss.

At a book show last night and there the
work stacked
upon the table like grocery lists
for the insane, obituaries
for the forgotten &
irrelevant. I arrived late
to my own event, got lost
on Magnolia Blvd
like I didn't grow up
there, but
I nearly forgot the flask &
was saved by my father, who
realized the inherent danger
of having to sign
books
and create instant wisdom
sober.

It rained the sky loose
like the analog static of a record player,
the valley gutters brimmed
and all my books sold. That's
an amazing thing, the books like
little children
holding the hands of others now
running to the car
in the rain. The flask was emptied
and the free beer as well.
Upon the keg change, the brew
was warm and all head
and no substance

like an infant.
Mike the poet stood
on the bar and shouted
his work, Rob Cohen circled
the room like a bullfighter
locked in the dream of
a child.

It was life consuming
life, art copying art,
death taking it straight on through
like the man you admire & wish
to emulate until
you look in the mirror.

They all stood around, the writers
and fans and artists and salon
stylists and people
who think they could be writers, and talked
literature like it still matters,
like they matter
and the dawn grieves
and James Dean asks again
for the 25 years he had. And a helmet.
I walked the rooms down
and smiled at people
I didn't know and smiled
at those I did. It goes on like this
at these things.
My son picked up the *Penis Pokey*
book thinking it a child's
and put his hand through the hole
and ran about the room. He played
imaginary soccer
on the sidewalk. I found myself
lecturing some poor fool

on how Sylvia Plath only
found the zero because
the housekeeper was late,
she was a careful one with her suicides,
and I
the literary asshole. Tobias refused
to wear a nametag in a shameless
rebellion against the act of art
while my wife
wore a short skirt & will find
a place in heaven for it. The books
dissipated like a storm
of black sparrows into the night,
signed & dated & wheeling & diving
in the rain.

The night was one to make me forget
the sadness of the moment,
the ache
where you can't even cry
that surrounds us.
Tonight my wife is downstairs
watching actors act as people
more than them
and I on this machine
working the game
the only way
I know
how.

Some nights it is worth it.

Three.

we all sit
& wait
for the beautiful
letdown.

tragedy badly done

The poets I know, whose number
fortunately
is few, regard me
as an oddity. They act as if
they enjoy the act
of struggling. They talk
of their writer's block,
their difficulties with jobs,
their former professors,
the spiritual decay around them.
They write poetry, and
very little of it
is readable, but 90%
(at least)
of everything is shit so
their output is neither
unexpected or
particularly
depressing.

They struggle to pay their bills
and struggle in their
relationships
& divorce each other
& beat each other
poorly
& sleep with each other
also poorly
& find parties with rooms
full of those who think they know
something you don't

& recite their poetry to anyone
who doesn't immediately
flee
& pretend to be interested in
my work. I don't pretend
likewise.

They have unkempt hair &
wear scarves even
in Los Angeles, listen
to bands you have never
heard of, carry books around
so others will notice. They
are actors in a part & the gods
are the casting directors, each
poet praying
for a bit of the magic.

My other friends hardly know
that I write poetry.
They wonder why I bother.
They have children and mortgages
due at the first of the month,
work for corporations, have
health care, do not wear scarves
and scorn ascots,
ask my advice on the spread
for the football games
this weekend.

I understand neither
of them. I am
the empty house screaming
at midnight, the drunk
scrambling
for the last drop,

the dusty photograph
in the basement. Riding
the miracle
headlong
in astonishment
it hasn't worn thin.
Writing the words and lines
guerilla
against the absurdity
given. It's the corner
I've backed into
without ever being
aware
there was one.

At Starbucks this morning
there was a young girl
amid the madness
behind the
counter. She was Indian,
or some approximation
thereof
& she bounced there
& about
full of the perfect
laughter
& smile enough
to fill the soul
of the empty.

The men in line
stood at attention
in front of her
and smiled, covering
their wedding rings
with their right hand
as they
ordered.

She exhibited none of
the inherent insanity
of her gender
yet.
The mood changes
& irrationality that have
laid centuries to waste

& given birth
to the screams caught
in the padding of madhouse
walls.

She is hiding
it. And I know this
and Junior knew it
and Buddy Guy knew it
and Buk knew it
and the wailing sparrow
knows it
and pity the man
who doesn't.
The one who thinks
he's got the
first,
the original,
the flower.

Men are violent
& simple, stupid
& horny, but transparent
as fishnets. Our attempts
at secrecy from
women
are comical.

I get my coffee
in line like a pawn
who will not
sacrifice
whatever limited
dignity is left.
They can have
her.

It goes to show
that history is the most
taught irrelevance on the
planet, that
we deserve
the misery
forthcoming
again
&
again.

I was 10 in the City of
Angels, the years of
madspring circuitous youth,
a time of instant sunshine
even when there was
none.
Being an only child
leaves you alone without
a brother to beat on, no sister
to tease & make cry. So you think,
you think more than you want to
and you finish
and look at the clock
and there
more time to think.

But this day a friend came over, all
relentless animal
energy and mindful
carelessness. We dressed in black and
wore beanies
and carried plastic guns
that did not look
plastic. Running about the neighborhood
alleys wishing
we were tough, pretending
we didn't have homes to go
home to
with loving parents.

We passed the sidewall of

an apartment complex &
the doors there. Spangled
sunlight angled down from
the overhang and the day was
new with laughter. Then a door opened
and an old lady
stood and raised a shotgun
we had convinced *her*, at least
and the twin bores there
like flared nostrils
& sound stopped
& time held
& I stared at the barrels
one to another. My friend
was behind me &
the lady said
like in a movie
"I know how to use this thing"
but she didn't use it
and the seconds rode on
like sitting on a stove
until
some primal instinct clicked
and we ran
like pinwheels in a tornado
Achilles could not have
made better time
in that alley.
I played football later and always
wished they had timed me
in the 40 on *that* day.

At home
we laughed at how big
the shotgun was compared
to her, about how if

92

she had fired it
she would have flown backwards
into her doorframe.
as if we would have seen it.
Thinking about
but never questioning
those to whom the gods
show mercy.

the body in the backyard

Neither of us grew up
and thus ran the summers down
like blown embers across
the desert floor, always westward,
in spooled heat &
graveyard boots.

Apartments where you slept
on the floor, you don't remember
them. I remember each.
Even some of the phone numbers.
I held you down the morning
you had your stomach pumped,
pried loose
the nail sunk to the bone.

I didn't know that I knew
how to dig a grave. After the overdose
I bent you into the fetal, and
buried you, and here, again,
under diction & the ripe weight
of words you never cared to hear.

I think of you now when I am drinking
in a coffee shop, alone. And
in thunderstorms. Certain songs,
you know how that is. Then you are
forgotten, and I am a body of
sparrows again chasing down
the
rain.

Gardenias & Porkpies
for Lady Day & Prez

Less than an hour from being plucked
& fingered the petals
wilt and yellow, thus
its reputation for one night stands,
the urgency of what memory reveals
in a song. Each of them leaned
towards their golden arm, their
lament
at the heart of things.

There are so many reasons
to tire of the mathematics of breathing,
the inevitable repetition and
lack of improvisation.
How form is but an ending.
And how the devil should tire for
the fun he is entitled. The only thing
not limiting enough,
the song in its entirety,
rages forth in gardenias &
porkpies in black & white
stills. Unable to say to one another
I have left you.
Unable to manage the humanity
of it all, leaving only
something more.

the closets are funhouses of
cleaning products & body parts
while the clothes
gather dust to hide the
bible.   There can be no
recompense from drunken
boxing with your wife.
Your son, perhaps.
Essays in philosophy are
breakfast menus with
pretension & the writers are still
writing all of it, the menus, the
poems, the novels, the instructions
on pizza boxes informing the masses
that said pizza must be
placed in the oven before
being eaten. The politicians are
wiping their bloody lips with
the American flag &
calling me a traitor. The soldiers die,
as they are supposed
to. Some white man in Arkansas or
California or Maine is hacking
up bodies of young women &
hiding them in barrels and covering them
in lyme to hide the smell, but I'm the
vulgar one for bringing
it up. His wife knows nothing
of this. I have heartburn & take
prilosec or pepcid or whatever
is at hand. The arch has dropped

on my right foot and shoes are
uncomfortable. The painters are looking
again
at their influences and wondering
where the magic went. The
masses wear WWJD bracelets &
cut each other
off on the freeway &
yell obscenities in the search
for meaning.
My son is sleeping soundly, fell
asleep tonight to Vivaldi.
Beware the ordinary, they know not
their capability.
Someone is watching you
at this moment. An airline pilot
is drunk over Bangkok
because his wife is sleeping with the insurance
agent
because he is never home
so he flies a plane for catharsis.
The TV is forever
absent & present. Downtown
(yours or mine)
a man is sleeping in a dumpster for warmth
wishing he had a reading light.
Dos is good for those times, perhaps
Lorca. A celebrity (names are
unimportant, they are interchangeable
like thermocouples in a heater)
is entering rehab publicly.
Someone is taking a picture
of it. Right now a 14 year old boy
is staring at the poster on his
wall of the woman wearing only
a bikini, the unattainable

madness, the prayer's
nubbed wick. And for just
this moment,
grace.

Life like a fishtail swinging
its rear about the bloated
corpses adrift in the quarter
the 9th Ward
the fallen elderly &
rudderless toddlers adorn
the camera like prizes.
I am wild with sadness,
a drunken ape battling
the madness throwing haymakers
at shadows.
It is that kind of night.

Anticipation has left the building
with desire, the living
without the living.
On television now the birthday party
in Iraq is all exploding candles
and cars and none of the
soldiers, the guardsmen, worries
much anymore about
missed trains or forgetting
their coat for the rain.
Each has forgotten how as a child
their mother & father would
notch the doorframe
like a kill
in pencil, each inch of progress
a doorway diminished
a step closer to loss.

The man on the screen
hair parted with a straightrazor
& camouflage shirt adorned with medals
& pins like a punk or mod
assures the viewing public
all patriotic americans
that soldier morale is at an alltime
high, that rebel insurgencies
are isolated occurrences, that
we are not there for
oil.
Thank goodness the commercials
follow
tell me what prescription drugs
to take and which cars to buy
because
it is so much easier when they
tell us what to do
and most of us do it
and the rest
need the mandate to pound
their head against
and shout
blind slogans without teeth.
We are all children given guns
& pills & bombs & bodies failing
throwing temper tantrums
and disciplining our kids
for doing the same.

The shot sparrows
the caged gorillas
the release of skin & ink
that sheds itself
upon the crest of a tattoo.
The poet sits and waits

for inspiration
to thus vomit into the zero
and God yawns
through the centuries
of boredom.

From his window shook
the red banners like dragon tails
the spring wind from the south,
open barometer for desolate
fields of crops.

Chairman Mao seated at his desk
his eye first upon the sparrow
flown above the crushing
poor, below the sky
that would not rain. The revolution
without a war. Lives spill
from these things like
an upturned bowl of water.
The paper boats in the fountain
folded thus
candid in their beauty
& fragility. On his blotter,
two documents: the executive order,
the blank poem. His ink meditates
over both, and the children
on the street below
shake for fear of being raised
with politics
alone.

this is how today collapses into itself

When we lose the beauty
of the morning & her song,
when the wait at the post office
is twenty deep
& later
the shoelace breaks.

When the night sheds
tears for the centuries
of heartbreak & laughter
& ignorance.
When the room is spinning
because you are gutshot
on liquor
& the myths
are in
hiding.

When the silence of your own
making
laughs too loud
& the rest
buried in ache.

When the good fight
is semantics
& the power rests
in the victim.

When the USB chip
with the poems

falls into the
toilet
your reaching
futile.

When Algren
Buk
Alvin
Waits
McCarthy
Heaney
Lorca
sound dead.

When the young
girl's smile
brings only thoughts
of
consequence.

The hospitals are waiting
for us to die,
they will control who gets
the morphine, who is
allowed the ecstasy,
who dies
first. Whose insurance
is best.

Alert and waiting as the night
folds itself
inward. Matter is primarily
empty space, we are
mostly water, organized
religion wastes more lives
than

war.

I propose tomorrow
to run the day down
like a dog
& chew the entrails
of the moment
& scream astonishment
at what we
are
given.

1927
& the lessons afforded
there.
The Bronx.

Then Los Angeles & my father's
yellow bug choking about
the yellow afternoon of my
youth. The dulcet & diamond voice
called out then as now
as the springs beneath
the vinyl seat covers stuck
the skin & my father wouldn't
cut the engine at
gas stations while pumping
for fear
of never starting again.   On the
radio there would be a tale
of the ballplayer's younger
sister, poetic description of
the double play, a reference to *Les
Miserables*. My father would laugh
and rub his hand vertically
on the back of his head as is
his way & finish
pumping gas.

Then my grandfather
was put into
a home & the antiseptic there.
My grandmother committed then

to Vin, each day
listening to the games
the broken diamondtales
the lies
the hat full of tears
the nobility of competition
the history
like a conversation with the
fates themselves. I would go
to her apartment & his voice
was never
far. The radio, the television,
bled the man loose
upon the floor & ceilings
& the space between. I would talk
to my grandmother about
the Dodgers & the surrogate
grandfather.

I have heard that voice for 35 years
yet missed the move from
Brooklyn, the fervor of
Robinson,
Koufax & the perfect
Game in '65. Vin Scully is
on now in years, there is
nothing specific
missing but the timing
not what it was
once.
Unimaginable
but when it goes, the only voice
worth hearing for
the wisdom of sport, the city here
yes, this one
will stutter tears

will tremble & fear the
unraveling of more than
baseball.

Looking back at the
crash site
I feel nothing
but the past. How sobs resemble
laughter,
how I broke my nose
twice and painted blindly
with nimble strokes those
adjectives best left unsaid.
I did most of it right
and that is
my fault.

So easy now to run
until there's nothing left
and swing from myth
to myth.
The mirrors and years
piggyback so much nothing
into a weight shouldered
like consequence & memories
I forget, even those
I don't want to.
Like gutters clotted
with the refuse of winter.

I was Ken once, condom
mechanic in plastic disguise, toothless
from a sprinkler head
and a line drive
hidden

even among the hiding.

But everything bleeds—
we stitch it shut with
the angels repair and
cauterize the past
with fire.
We owe the centuries that.

And spring carries with it
the acrid smell of revolution
the blood on the teeth
the coming coup.
I learned then to compromise
my prayers and alibis,
those promises on which
I grew fond of pretending.

I keep the rain with me
now. It is enough.

slow
dogs trying desperately to make sense
of the sky & the pews worn smooth
amid the despair that follows
victory. I've yet to meet
an interesting person truly
heavenbound pursuant to said guidelines
set forth in the throat of laughter
too loud
for confessional. It's in our nature
to hate the ending
the cliché unmet, how
the final act must conclude
what was introduced in the first.
The room is on fire, even the blind
see that. It's our reaction
that makes up the day, that
uncorks the bottle & sets the neighbor
aflame.

marching backwards

The stars are no company tonight
and I nailed to
the roof of the world
and I feel no blame
for the behavior
concerning an apple
and a snake, the lack
of our evolution, apes
in cotton. We deserve
the worst of it
though
the deserving will be
the last to receive it,
to drink their sum.

There is marching on my street
in parades of rank & file
all lockstep drumbeat and
capped smiles of some other
infinity. They hold their torches
aflame, the flag aloft
like violence, an
altar of blood upon which
we sup our sweet fruits
and stroke our erect baton
of nationalism.

I have left my heart behind
he is a stranger
to ceremony. Credit the commies
for the existence of god

in our schools,
the iron of fate
to beguile fools. Through it all,
I am afraid
       of the masses.
Old soldier crow teeters
on a wire above the street
and watches the humans pass.
As do I. They have united
to burn the intellectuals
tonight
needing something to ignite &
justify the holy tailoring
of a noose. I want to shout
to them in passing: *The man who preaches*
needs it more than you! but
I stay hidden instead. Mom
always said I burn easily.

Let's call it rebellion, darling
when we loathe the very humanity
that calls sunshine a miracle
and fanaticism sanity.
Marching backwards from
our point of origin,
gallows ahead
&
gallows behind.

blue sky today as the bombs stack
about us, the windstrength of
the heavens can do nothing for us
the bloody stars
the alone & astonished
the universe hemmed in by our
stupidity. People come to my house
& talk of their outfit &
the small difficulties of their days
while the soundtrack plays
muted about our lives for another
to hear. The car bombs, the handheld,
those buried in the soil, those
worn as a vest, those dropped from planes
amid the Gregorian chants of
eunuch monks as
we pound nails
through the hours
given.

The line between now &
forever is fishingline thin, the days full
of dance & aces. The politicians
teach us subtraction through
war, irony through
patriotism. The miracle
of illusion by blood & by
love, death being
the opposite of time.
I don't know what to tell these
people except

the bombs are the kiss
we held too long. I think
your outfit looks great, I say,
to he & she & nobody
& think of the bombs
being created
this moment, to kill
the children of
children.

they expect it, history
is the lesson
heeded by those who will
send you to death
happily
for a profit.
Not enough,
the agony of everyday,
but
still they sell you
teamwork
training
patriotism
and the values of
freedom.
Never mind the dying
for (their) profits!
Where is your
loyalty? Your decency?
Are you not
proud to be
American?
Their rhetoric
is your
death,
the folded flag,
the casket surrounded
by soil & young
dead fools.

rings in the pawn shop

The wind & the rain
whores loosed
upon the night
raw themselves against
that which we build
to protect
the innards, the
scattershot soul never
found but
there
nonetheless.
& thank the gods
for
these walls.

I sit & drink & listen
to *Orphans*
&
wait for the rejection
notices & wonder
why?
Another pencilnotch
on the doorframe
to show mom
how I've grown, another
asshole approves
or
more likely doesn't
and for what? I look at
their choices,
too careful

or
affected eclecticism,
and the slow waltz
between.

The sparrow has folded
his wings & ducked
his head from the
rain tonight.

Two books out now, a third
on the way. A stack
of litmags
dreadful & nearly so
containing poems
like children graduated
and many not. But I am proud
of the dropouts
as well, they
will find work
as plumbers,
circus freaks,
politicians.

But the single malt
says hello
&
Tom sings ballads
&
we all sit &
wait for
the beautiful
letdown.

I tried my hat at whatever filled the day, libraries,
films, drinking, innocence like
privilege before the wailing sparrow
began to eat at the solitude. The live-in
girlfriend who worked at marketing
and pretended to understand.
Bless her soul & the beer she brought home,
her mother
the alcoholic counselor & obsessed
debutante. I hung on the outskirts
of the city, the bars,
Andy's, poolhalls, taking the drinks
as they came.

I was always surprised that my academic
pedigree
didn't guarantee me anything
but a smile
& still I worked the seams of
arrogance until the drinks
stopped coming, the friends fewer
&
more demanding on their returns. It was a run
not a good one
but one nonetheless that inspired
the likes of poetry & the disease
of this page
this computer
this need.

Tom & I finishing bottles of Jack

in the backyard past
the point the innocence
left. I was not good to them, any
of them, but most are not good
to one another. I was not
exceptional in that way or
any other despite
my faith
that the gods were listening
that I was deserving of anything
besides
derision. I was charming enough
to get by,
to peddle the wares like a whore
to sling coffee behind
a counter for beer money
and pool bets. The relationship fell apart
because the joke had staled
and I moved back to LA and its
womb. Another girl there
(bless her soul), more coffee,
poems born of spite & fear
and blind encouragement though none
was deserved. People continued
to see the good in me
in spite of myself. I sent the poems off
and learned lessons on
the machinery of failure
&
the rejections were crushing, then
difficult, then expected.
Finally they were
laughable. I read what their journals
contained and sneered at
their choices. They did not wail
they had no balls

no guerilla. They were
careful & technical
& at best
made you
smirk.

LA was the testing ground
& the drinking
I controlled
& work improved
(the suits saw potential)
& the poems improved
(the professor saw potential)
& I no longer slouched
towards the given fate but
flicked it off with both
hands skyward & immersed
the work in the genius
of others.

I haven't evolved from there.
Others say what they will
but
the wailing sparrow thunders
about the sky
&
the work now includes novels
and these little poems
&
the beating heart of blue
marigolds.

The edges of rainbows are
sharp like the teeth of the morning
in winter here, like
Sunday's vacant faith
& despite
their mythic and obvious qualities,
the ties colored into
bled amalgams, the castiron
pots twist the after rainfall
hallucinations
like the logic of a child.
That's the rub,
you will learn to hate
mirrors, the pots
empty or filled
with the perverse
dreams of the selfish &
unimaginative. At best.
The wise men hide in
their fragile reputation
&
the poets
hide in form &
terminology & ascots. Thus
the unexplainable loss,
the insignificance of
trying.

The mercy we wish to find
has become
the propaganda of

bureaucrats
&
it's hard not to feel
like an asshole
believing in something clearly
not available, like the desperate
kid you knew in school
looking to score with the
supermodel
on his wall. & when
you leave a message
for the gods
they play back a
laugh track, so
you must know,
as I do: best to
give it a roar,
burn
the eyes in the sun,
flip the tables & smash
the mirrors.
Never come morning
will come
without your permission
riding the backs
of rainbows
whispering the logic
of a child
in nursery rhymes
you recognize
but can't quite
place.

the unforgivable search for grace

Have mercy for
the descent has begun again
on this chair, this
night. The truth is beneath
the concrete
the sunset
the poesy
the endless chatter against the
unforgiving hours. The mirror
lies like
a camera, the eye sees what
it wants, the lover sees
himself, the truth is
the halo of crows at dusk,
the spontaneous dance at
RiteAid in front of the
sunglass rack.

It will find you at times when
you have given up
the search.

The old professor has been fired
for his mishandling of
funds, interestingly enough
not for his mishandling
of others. He was ruthless
& beautiful & tiny in his
arrogance & taught me
everything I needed
to know & then

forget
about poetry. Pentameter &
historicity & the seamless
world of Eliot & the confessionals
&
the deep image subjectivists &
the breath line & the
suicides
&
womanizing
&
the careful architecture of linebreaks.

Levine was dismissed because
he didn't like LA but
Heaney was a pal & Dylan too &
Buk
wasn't worth discussion
somehow.

We all seek
an audience, I don't
blame him
for that. But the
discovery
of truth is dark for most, and
for others, darker still.

An old friend of mine stood
in line at the local 7/11 last week
and held the items he was to pay
for. He teased his boy next
to him and smiled at his wife, complained
briefly
of a chest pain beyond his 36 years
and collapsed there
like the strings had been cut
never to stand again. Dead
before the ambulance
arrived at the hospital. Nothing for that,
those moments left
the gods bestow & smear the walls
crimson with the holy.

The most brilliant man whose time
I shared is in & out of
madhouses
with a regularity most share
with drunken nights or
midnight liaisons. The fools carry on
in carnal bliss, nevermind
the hours bearing down to
burrow & hide alone
that which we do not wish to give.

The women past
gone to eat the red night, dolls
of such mindful
insanity, I wonder at times

126

what they think now.
Then it passes.
Decades gone, those moments
of immortality and endless
night. Now the hours don't
shine right, the wailing sparrow
rages in impotent glory, the
skin which coats the bone
folds against the assailing
gravity.

The nights in the apartment in
Concord, madness & liquor & the cooler
that doubled as a coffee table. Nothing better
than laying on my bed staring at
the popcorn ceiling & the hell of
possibility. Alone. They still came by
then, the women & the friends & men
with pinched faces and eyes full
of a smallness & hatred for anything
other than them. Still,
I have forgotten most things. I cannot
get them back.

History has taught us nothing, that
is the lesson for today. That the
ignorance we are born with far
exceeds that which we will pound
the earth with. We pass it along like
a venereal disease and are proud to have
shared it, proud to have licked
the diamond clean
once again.

So many words I have
choked on. Either cowardice or

circumstance or ridiculous
optimism. They have us by the
jugular as the life
burns away & some of us
clutch the piece they cannot
have. Others give it away
blissfully.

I will get up tomorrow, look
in the mirror & recognize
nothing. Being a fool is normal.
More creases will have set in
across the land, more soldiers
will be dead. More lies will
be told &
more people will believe them.
The interesting will die for
others to wonder
at such impossibilities of fate
while the rest will think of
nothing whatsoever.
And
despite the injustice & foolish masses,
despite pop songs &
the death of children,
the wailing sparrow of blue ruin
will soar in a shock of
joy
in the face of its
opposite.

                              the
            Sonny Haynes
                   poems.

    7 of diamonds.   Flick.
    Ace of clubs. Flick.

deep song (a Sonny Haynes joint)

The sunlight ran in pinstripes from
the blinds in the
motel room, the cigarette smoke
alive in the folds. I
flicked playing cards
across the emptiness for
lack of a better thing
to do, waiting
for the arrival of
savage night.

Queen of hearts. Flick.
Jack of spades. Flick. Drag.
The opened ground there, the
distance afforded
one another.

The .45 at my side like
the afterbirth you
can't stand to throw
away. I spoon it into
my mouth, get the feel
of the thing,
the metallic rinse
against the teeth.

7 of diamonds. Flick.
Ace of clubs. Flick.
Vegas awaits. The city that
doesn't sleep & me with eyes
incapable of closing.

Drag.
Awaiting the
darkness.

the road to Vegas (a Sonny Haynes joint)

Plan B
had gone according to
plan, the burning
& the cash in the trunk. The cabin
would still be aflame, orange embers
tossed into the stinking night
of flesh & gamble.
The smoke from my smoke
curled like a tail
out the window & into the
Nevada dark. The Four Roses bottle lay on
the vinyl seat beside me,
some icon of failure. I said
to nobody at all: The wagon
is the lowest turn
of the wheel, when a man
sees the truth and a lie is
needed. The collapse of hope
in the virus of life. The bourbon
answered. And again.

Even God's asshole gets reception
thus
the Gerald Wilson Orchestra played
Cruisin With Cab
& the open windows bared themselves
in an attempt to offer
the desert something
besides sand. The .38
sat beside the bottle
like a picture.

Another hundred miles to Vegas & the black past
followed.

The Mobil station was lit as stars
frozen in place. The Pegasus stalled
in departure on the sign as
I pulled up to the pump. The clerk
was listening to Bing on the wireless
& stood when I approached.
How much, Buddy, he asked &
stared at the sparrow in flight
on my neck. I unhinged my
snapcap & slicked back the hair
underneath. I believe I'll burn
5 bucks, Chief, I said. Is that a sparrow
or a swallow? He asked.
Beg pardon. Me.
I mean, I hear they look alike, &
I was wonderin. Him.
It's the wailing sparrow of blue ruin—he's
the one who kills people, not
me.
I smiled at him & he saw something
there enough to stop asking questions.
5 bucks it is, pal. Him.
I walked out
of the shop & there
the weeping of the planet
bent on scabrous knees in
the dust. Nothing
for that.

I pumped my gas & then took
a piss on the mercycracked platelets
behind the shop. In midstream
I heard the siren some mile

or two off in the flat soundstage
of hardpack. My first thought was the .38
in the passenger seat
of the Merc.

I walked back to my ride like
I'm not wanted for
Multiple murders or the 95 grand in
cash in the trunk. That is not
easy.
I lit a cigarette & reached for the
bottle, slugged a draught of the bourbon. They
were coming from Vegas.
That was okay. One way was better than two.

I sat & smoked & considered the possibility of
dying in a gas station
in Nevada & again considered
where the good times had gone.
Instead I dropped the car into gear
in expectation &
curled my fingers about the rod. They arrived
like an American Parade, red&blue lights flashing
in the panic of a flag, tires skidding
across the dirt. They took their positions behind
their open doors
and one guy started shouting instructions
into the bullhorn loud
enough to make the deaf wince,
COME OUT WITH YOUR HANDS UP! THERE
IS NO NEED
FOR BLOODSHED HERE! COOPERATE &
NOBODY
GETS HURT.
The clerk came out from the front door of the shop
with his hands grasped behind

his head. I knew that punk looked
shady.
I mean, what kind of question was that?

I revved the beast beneath me
& rolled it towards Vegas.

like baseball (a Sonny Haynes joint)

The red garter swung in the loose rhythm
of neon, its delirium stain
blurring the motel wall. The man tied
in the chair looked like life
were winter only. A lifetime
of snow. The Four Roses bottle
atop the table. Sonny in the chair
opposite.

"Baseball is important. It stays
in the thoughts. Like, you know how
you're supposed to think about
baseball
when you're trying to hold out?
You know…"
The man looked as if
he didn't. Sonny continued,
"Anyways, it's the same with
the knee. You come down with
a tomahawk, throw the hands
forward, keep the weight centered,"
he demonstrated with his
hands, grabbed the bottle & tipped
it vertical. The ruins dribbled
down his chin.

"My daddy taught me to hit," Sonny
reflected. "Don't imagine he
intended it to be used this way
but life sure surprises the shit outta me.
You?" The man strained his

neck & looked away. Snail tracks
on his cheeks. Sonny ripped
the tape off his mouth &
smiled. "Any
last words?"

The man looked down &
shuddered. Vomited on his lap. The
room exploded in
the sour remains. "Really?" Sonny
answered. "A whole life & nothing
to say?" Sonny slicked his hair
back with his hand & took
another draught. "Okay then. Think
about baseball. You never know.
It works for me." Sonny stood &
handled the bat leaned
against the wall. The red neon
splashed.

About.

born & raised in LA.
degrees from UC Berkeley & USC.
wife & son.
guerillalit.
scotch.
working on novel. noir.